Sensational full-color photographs and a carefully researched tale take young readers on a fascinating journey beneath the waves to explore a mysterious world.

"Exquisite full-color photographs and text packed with information introduce middle grade readers to the underwater world of the kelp forest…an excellent resource for the study of sea life."
—*Booklist*

"The full-color photographs are of unusually high quality and detail and are artistically arranged, skillfully complementing the text. Wu's obvious love for and sensitivity to his subject make this superior to similar titles." —*School Library Journal*

"The next generation of marine biologists will be sleeping with this book under their pillows." —*Smithsonian*

Book design by Laura Jane Coats.

Printed in Hong Kong

Library of Congress

Cataloging-in-Publication Data:

Wu, Norbert.

Beneath the Waves / by Norbert Wu.

Summary: Describes plants and animals that live

in and around kelp bed forests, including otters,

seals, plankton, eels and octopi. Includes index.

hc ISBN: 0-87701-835-9

pb ISBN: 0-8118-1808-X

1. Kelp bed ecology–Juvenile literature.

(1. Kelp bed ecology. 2. Marine animals.

3. Marine plants. 4. Ecology.) I. Title

QH541.5.K4W8   1992

574.5'2636–dc20   91-29652

2CIP   AC

Distributed in Canada by Raincoast Books

8680 Cambie Street, Vancouver,

British Columbia V6P 6M9

10 9 8 7 6 5 4 3 2 1

Chronicle Books

85 Second Street

San Francisco, California 94105

Website: www.chronbooks.com

John Steinbeck wrote of Ed Ricketts, a biologist of Monterey,

Children on the beach he taught how to look for
and find beautiful animals in worlds they had not
suspected were there at all.

This is the purpose of this book: to help children discover
beauty and life in a world they may otherwise not know of at all.

Norbert Wu, Orinda, California, August 1991.

Beneath the
WAVES

Exploring the Hidden World
of the Kelp Forest

Written and photographed by

N O R B E R T   W U

chronicle books · san francisco

***To Deanna,
who knows me better than
anyone else and accepts me
for what I am.***

Acknowledgements: Photography, particularly underwater photography, requires the help, support, and advice of many people. Spencer Yeh, Matt Murphy, and Sam Shabb braved many a day of cold water and few rewards, as did Howard Hall, Bob Cranston, and Mark Conlin. Dr. James Watanabe and Charles Baxter helped nurture my interest in marine life and photography while at Hopkins Marine Station. The folks at Bob Davis Camera Shop in La Jolla and Orinda Camera were continually helpful with their handling of my film. Cindy Sagen and Phyllis Winston at the Monterey Bay Aquarium have been supportive and important editors of my work; without them and other photography researchers, I would not be able to make a living doing what I do best. Thanks also goes to the folks at Point Lobos Marine Reserve for allowing me to spend a summer there and to Leon Hallacher and Henry Kaiser who showed me their special areas. Sam and Ange lent continuing support and diversion during my long days in the office. Victoria Rock at Chronicle Books encouraged this book and pulled it together through all its stages.

Introduction

Hidden beneath the waves is another world. Instead of air, its atmosphere is water. Instead of winds and storms, it is ruled by tides and currents. Like our world, this underwater realm has its forests, canyons, mountains, and streams. It is filled with creatures, small and large, fast and slow, darting, dancing, singing, gliding, hunting, grazing, and mating. Here in this hidden world are anemones, their petals tipped with deadly poisons. Sea slugs, sporting neon-bright colors, crawl through dark forests. Fish swoop after their prey, like swallows feeding upon insects. Sparks fly from luminescent plankton as dolphins swim through the water. Jellyfish, too, give off bursts of light when they are disturbed.

Like us, the creatures of the sea can only catch a glimpse of the other world. Their sky ends abruptly. We call it the surface, but to the creatures of this hidden world, it is a ceiling. It is the boundary where the creatures of the sea and land meet. It has only been in recent decades, with the invention of SCUBA in 1943, that humans have been able to cross this boundary and enter the spectacular world of the deep sea.

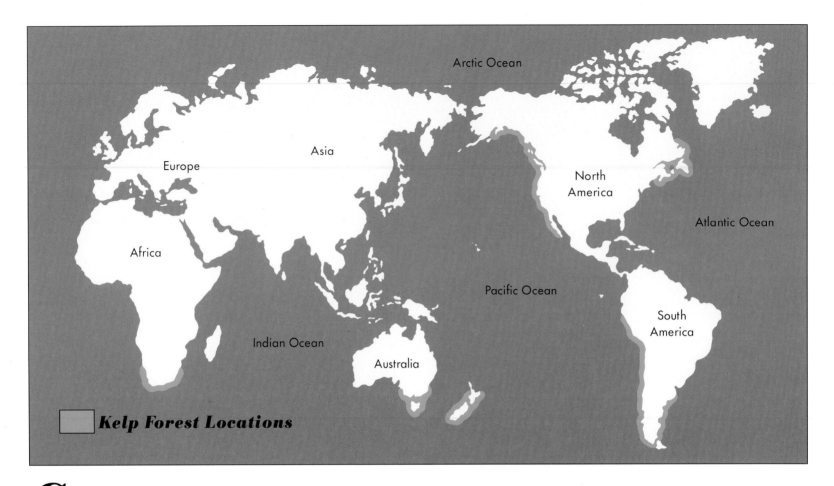

Kelp Forest Locations

Graceful, lush, and vibrant kelp forests can be found along the coasts of several continents. They decorate the Pacific coast of North America from Alaska to Baja, and the Atlantic coast from Maine to Cape Cod. They also can be found off the shores of South America, South Africa, and southern Australia. Along the coast of California alone, twenty different species of kelp flourish.

The beauty and the bounty of the kelp forest is far richer than most people know. For hundreds of years, people around the world have used kelp as a food source. Today, it is harvested for iodine, potassium, and other minerals and vitamins. A natural gel called algin is also obtained from kelp, and is used in everyday items such as ice cream, pudding, medicines, and salad dressing.

Kelp forests can be found around the world. In order for kelp to grow, it needs a hard surface on which to attach its holdfast, water that is clear and cool (kelp grows best in water not warmer than seventy degrees Farenheit) as well as rich in nutrients, and moderate water movement.

Because kelp forests are teeming with sea life, they attract commercial fishermen in search of shellfish and fish to sell in the marketplace. Still others, like SCUBA divers, are drawn to the graceful and wondrous world of the kelp forest to enjoy its never-ending beauty and marvelous secrets.

Waves that wash over the kelp plant are good because they contain gases and other nutrients, but waves that are too rough will tear the kelp plants.

S.C.U.B.A. stands for Self-Contained Underwater Breathing Apparatus. While the name sounds complicated, SCUBA diving is actually very easy to learn. Thousands of people from age ten to age eighty have learned to dive.

Most divers go through a full course of instruction which can last from one to eight weeks. During this training, divers learn how to put on gear underwater, to clear a mask that has been flooded, and to breathe from a tank. They also learn to dive safely and to have respect for the underwater environment.

*A*long the coast, the day is starting. The sun slowly rises, revealing the steep cliffs bordering the cold ocean. Light begins to filter down through the kelp forest that lies hidden beneath the waves.

Silhouetted against the rising sun, a noisy oyster-catcher walks along the water's edge, calling loudly. It spots a limpet, crawling toward its home on a rock. With a peck of its thick, red beak, the oystercatcher dislodges the limpet, turns it over, and picks out the meat.

A great blue heron glides above the water, heading for a log that is caught among the kelp at the water's surface. The heron has fished from this log for the past two weeks. Once perched on the log, it holds so still that that it almost looks like part of the log. A rockfish or one of the many crabs that live below in the kelp forest will soon be snapped up by the heron's long, thin bill.

Oystercatchers search the shoreline for food. They use their thick red bills to crack open shells and get at the animals inside.

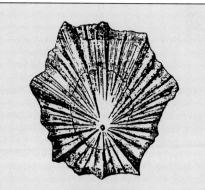

Limpet

A limpet is a snail with a cone-like shell. Like squids and octopi, it is a member of the mollusk family. Limpets are excellent rock-clingers, and are virtually impossible to detach from their rock homes unless they are caught by surprise — before their one muscular foot can seal to the stone. Some limpets have homes to which they constantly return. They make their homes by scraping a shallow pit in a rock with the edge of their shells, and wedging themselves in tightly. The limpet will leave its crevice to graze algae on rocks, sometimes wandering up to three feet or more before returning to its home.

Above: Herons and other sea birds hunt for small fish and crabs that live in the kelp canopy.

Right: This kelp crab has covered itself with a piece of drift kelp in an attempt to hide from predators.

As the sun climbs higher, the sounds of the day begin to rise over the constant crashing of the waves. A seagull squawks a greeting. Along the shore, a herd of sea lions is basking in the morning sun.

A sea otter splashes in the shallow water near the beach, diving up and down, up and down, fishing for its breakfast. Eventually it comes up with a kelp crab, which it quickly devours. Then the otter floats on the water's surface, rolling in the kelp and combing its fur with its paws. It does this after every meal, and it is this constant grooming that keeps the otter's fur clean, fluffy, and full of air.

A sudden snort startles the otter. It looks up to see a pair of large, black eyes peeking out of the water. It is a harbor seal. The seal snorts, either in fear or playfulness, then sinks below the surface.

Above: Sea lions are noisy, social animals that gather together in large groups.

Left: Unlike sea lions, harbor seals are very shy and they don't bark.

Sea otters do not have blubber to keep them warm in the water. Instead, their fur traps a layer of air which acts as insulation. If caught in an oil spill, they soon die from the cold because their fur cannot hold the layer of air.

Below: Urchins and sea stars are both members of a group of animals called echinoderms.

The sea otter dives again, and this time finds one of its favorite foods: a large sea urchin. The otter rolls onto its back and uses its flat stomach as a table. With nimble paws, it pries open the sea urchin, carefully avoiding the urchin's long, sharp spines. Then the otter drops the urchin's shell into the sea.

A school of señorita fish, patrolling the waters beneath the canopy, follows the shell's path as it twists and turns its way to the rocky ocean bottom. Here bright orange garibaldi, California sheephead, and rockfish fight over the otter's urchin. Even bat sea stars slowly glide over the rocks and sand to see what remains of the feast.

Kelp rivals bamboo as the world's fastest growing plant. During the summer, it can grow as much as two feet per day.

Below: The sea otter finds almost all its food within the kelp forest.

It is dark underneath the kelp canopy, like a forest with bits of golden light shimmering through the branches. Like a forest on land, the kelp forest is home to many animals. Some spend their entire lives within the kelp environment. Others visit the forest looking for food or protection. But the kelp plant is not a tree. It is a type of algae, and its "roots" and "leaves" are very different from those of a tree. Like a tree, the kelp plant depends on sunlight to grow. During the summer, when the sun shines brightly, the kelp grows quickly. During the winter, however, storms can tear up the forest by uprooting the kelp plants.

The "leaves" of the kelp plant are called blades. They are rubbery and have bulbs that support the blades and help them grow toward the sun.

Photosynthesis

Stretching toward the sun, the blades at the top of the plant spread out along the water's surface to collect as much sunlight as they can. The plant uses the sunlight's energy to make food by combining carbon dioxide (a gas) with water that is absorbed by the plant. This food-making process is called photosynthesis.

The "trunks" are called stipes. These hollow tubes transport food from the blades at the top of the plant down to the holdfast at the bottom.

The rootlike structures are called holdfasts. They spread themselves on top of rocks and anchor the plant. Without the holdfast, the plant would be washed ashore.

When hungry sea urchins invade a kelp forest, the result is an undersea desert called a "sea urchin barrens." Without predators to control their numbers, huge populations of sea urchins can destroy entire kelp forests.

Below: Sea urchins destroy kelp forests by eating only the base of the plant, leaving the rest to float away.

Storms are not the only threat faced by kelp forests. In some areas, population explosions of sea urchins have created "sea urchin barrens." In these areas, sea urchins have grown out of control and there is not enough food to feed them all. Generally, sea urchins feed by scraping algae off of rocks, but when their algae supply is depleted, they will turn to eating kelp plants. The result is an undersea desert where once there was a lush forest. Scientists think that sea otters may help keep the urchin populations in check, thus preventing "deforestation" and helping to maintain healthy kelp forests.

*S*ea otters were almost driven to extinction in the 1800's by the demand for their thick furs. But in 1911, several countries banded together to regulate the hunting of otters. Today, it is illegal to kill or even bother a sea otter, and thousands of otters can be found along the Pacific Coast. While sea otters may be unpopular with fishermen because they eat sea urchins and abalone, it is lucky for the kelp forest and many of the animals that depend on it that sea otters have such healthy appetites.

Sea otters play an important role in keeping kelp forests healthy by eating sea urchins before the urchins eat the kelp.

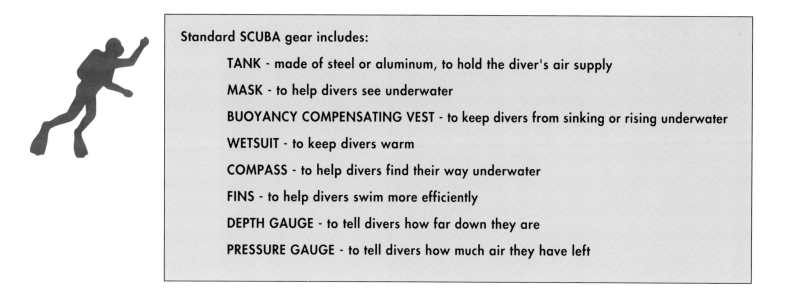

Standard SCUBA gear includes:

TANK - made of steel or aluminum, to hold the diver's air supply

MASK - to help divers see underwater

BUOYANCY COMPENSATING VEST - to keep divers from sinking or rising underwater

WETSUIT - to keep divers warm

COMPASS - to help divers find their way underwater

FINS - to help divers swim more efficiently

DEPTH GAUGE - to tell divers how far down they are

PRESSURE GAUGE - to tell divers how much air they have left

Left: Jellyfish can grow to be gigantic, sometimes taller than three people.

Below: Some jellyfish can travel under their own power by squeezing their bodies so water is forced out of the open end of the bell, slowly propelling the jellyfish along.

On the edge of the kelp forest, a school of jellyfish passes by. Jellyfish are called drifters because they travel by drifting with the ocean's currents. When found washed up on the beach, jellyfish look like small blobs. But when seen in their natural habitat, floating gracefully through the water, they are quite beautiful.

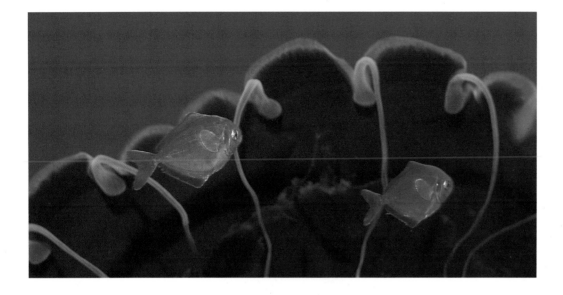

Above: Juvenile jacks are good at avoiding the jellyfish's tentacles and use them as a barrier between themselves and their predators.

Left: The medusafish wraps itself in the jellyfish's stinging tentacles when it is frightened.

When jellyfish drift into the kelp forest they become entangled, making a fine meal for bat stars and other kelp forest residents.

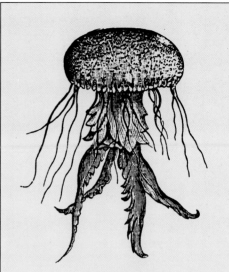

Jellyfish

Much about these unusual animals is a mystery. We do know that jellyfish aren't fish at all. They are a primitive animal called a coelenterate, which is Latin for "body cavity." Like anemones, sea fans, and coral, jellyfish have a central body, called a bell, which is surrounded by a string of stinging tentacles. Jellyfish have no heart, no brain, no bones, and no fins. In fact, they are made up almost entirely of water.

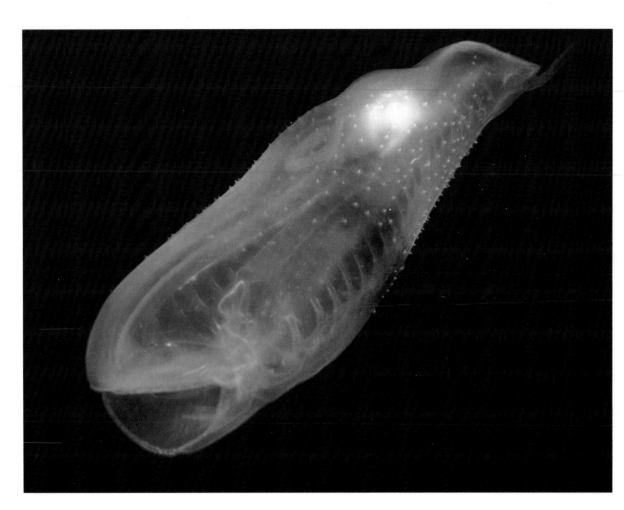

A pelagic salp glides by with its mouth open, gulping large quantities of water. The water is then filtered for food particles.

Below: Amphipods are small crustaceans. They are the "insects"of the marine world and, like flies and ants on land, they are eaten by many different kinds of animals.

There are many other animals at the edge of the kelp forest. The waters here are rich in tiny, microscopic life called plankton. Although it is invisible to the human eye, plankton, which consists of tiny plants, young fishes, crabs, and larvae, supports all other life in the ocean. A foot-long salp, looking like a miniature whale, glides through the water with its mouth open, gulping in large quantities of water. The middle of the salp's body is lined with muscles that contract and suck in water which is then filtered for food particles. A small amphipod has taken up residence within the salp's body and feeds off the food particles brought in by the salp.

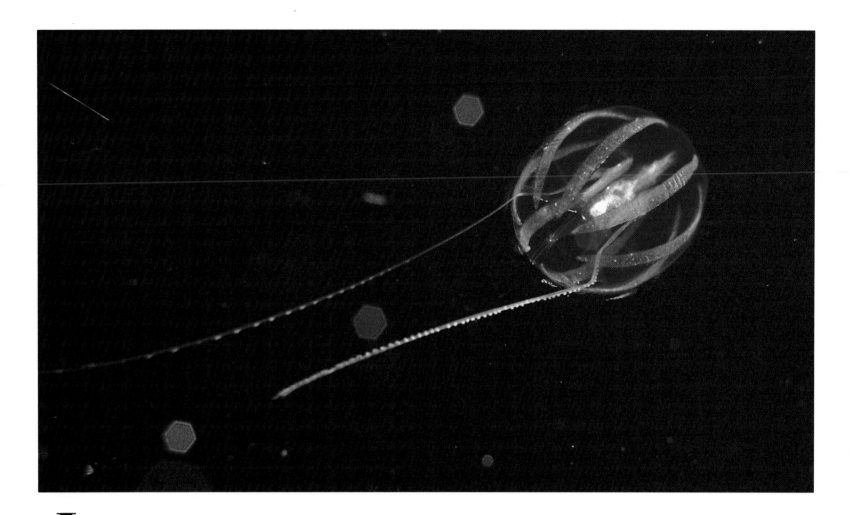

Jellyfish and comb jellies float by, looking like tiny jewels. One type of comb jelly, the sea gooseberry, trails sticky tentacles behind it, gathering plankton. When it has collected enough food, it stuffs its tentacles into its stomach and wipes them clean.

The sea gooseberry swims by vibrating its "comb rows," which are hairlike projections along its body. The comb rows reflect light at different angles, creating a rainbow effect.

There are limits to how long a SCUBA diver can stay at a given depth. Traditionally, divers have calculated these times using dive tables on land. Now dive computers, which divers carry into the water with them, are used. Because these computers adjust to the diver's actual depth, they are more accurate than dive tables.

Inside the kelp forest, turban and top snails crawl among the stipes, feeding on the dead and rotting parts of the plants. Kelpfish peer out from behind the blades and stipes using their body shape and color to blend into the background. A shy, tiny clingfish holds tightly to a kelp stipe with a small suction cup on its belly. It looks remarkably like the stipe, and like the kelpfish, it uses this camouflage for safety.

Top snails have a row of rasping, file-like teeth, called radula, that cannot pierce a healthy kelp plant. They feed on the dead and rotting parts of the plant.

Lingcods can grow to be four feet long. Because they blend in so well with the rocks of the ocean floor, they are master ambush hunters who use their camouflage to surprise prey.

Below: This colorful Catalina blenny is about as big as a human thumb.

On the rocks below, a large lingcod sits very still, watching carefully. Its body is green and blotched in a pattern that makes it blend into the rocks. A tiny, brightly colored Catalina blenny also watches for bits of food drifting by in the current. The bright colors of the Catalina blenny probably warn of its unpleasant taste.

The rockfish grows to be about ten inches long. This rockfish is flaring its gills to scare off intruders.

*A*t the bottom of the kelp forest, many faces peer out from between the rocks. A gopher rockfish maintains its territory. Nearby, a *Pisaster* sea star has found a volcano limpet. The sea star grasps the limpet with its many sticky tube feet, but the limpet quickly releases a white mantle from underneath its shell. The mantle is so slippery that the sea star can't hold on, and the limpet soon glides away to safety.

A mantle is a fleshy cape that lies underneath the shell of a mollusk. It produces a chemical that builds up in layers to form the shells of mollusks. Below, the slippery mantle saves a limpet from becoming the meal of a hungry sea star.

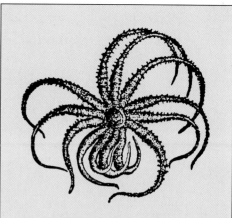

Sea Stars

Sea stars have arms that radiate from a central disk. The arms are called rays, and while most sea stars have five rays, some have as many as forty-five. The rays are used for traveling and hunting. If a ray breaks off, the sea star will grow a new one. If part of the central disk breaks off with the ray, an entirely new sea star may grow. This process is called regeneration, and can take from a month to a year, depending on the species.

*A*s soon as the limpet settles down, another sea star, a very large *Pycnopodia* sun star, glides near. The sun star moves much faster than the *Pisaster* did, and within a few seconds it is gone, leaving the limpet to resume grazing on the algae and invertebrate cover of the rock.

There are more than 600 species of starfish in the world. The *Pycnopodia* sun sea star, shown here, is the largest of all and can grow to be three feet across.

This *Pisaster* comet is just beginning to grow new arms.

The wolf eel is not an eel at all. It is more closely related to the blenny. One of its favorite foods is the sea urchin.

Below: A moray eel. Eels look like snakes, but in reality they are long, bony fish.

The rocks that have tumbled from the steep cliffs to the coastline rest on the ocean floor, forming dark, mysterious caves. In one small cave, a six-foot-long wolf eel peers out. It is a very ferocious-looking fish, but in fact it can be very friendly. It is one of the few underwater creatures that stays with a single mate for life.

In another cave, a moray eel keeps watch. Unlike other fish, moray eels don't have gills. Instead they breathe through their mouths. Because of this, their mouths are almost constantly open, which makes moray eels seem more ferocious than they really are.

Throughout the kelp forest, bright orange garibaldi fish are tending their nests. The garibaldis' favorite sites are among the rocks that litter the ocean floor. Here they farm patches of rock, making sure that only a particular kind of algae grows. They pick unwanted kinds of algae off their rocky nests with their mouths, and if another creature tries to move into the nest, the garibaldi will chase it away or even carry it away in its mouth.

Garibaldis

The males of this species are the housekeepers. They do the farming, and in the spring and summer when the female lays the eggs, it is the male that keeps the nest clean and safe from predators. Once the female has laid the eggs, the male fertilizes them and watches over them until they hatch two weeks later. The babies are born covered with blue dots and are quickly carried away to new areas by the ocean's currents.

A garibaldi fish tends his nest.

The cliffs along the coastline form underwater walls covered with anemones, hydrocorals, and other invertebrate life.

Below: Each stripe of color on the rock wall consists of thousands of identical anemones, called clones, all of which likely descended from a single ancestor.

Big red anemones — flowerlike creatures — and sea stars blanket the rocky bottom, and the walls are covered with hundreds of brightly colored anemones jammed together, forming stripes of orange, red, and purple. Although they look like flowers, the slow-moving anemones are actually animals — coelenterates, like the jellyfish.

Left: Each anemone is shaped like a hollow sac, with a mouth surrounded by a ring of stinging tentacles. They will pull in their tentacles if bothered, or when digesting a meal.

Below: Anemones will eat almost anything that falls within their reach. Here, an anemone has caught a piece of drift kelp.

Anemones

Even though they look like flowering plants, anemones are actually animals. They protect themselves and capture food with stinging cells in their tentacles. They will consume anything that falls within reach of their waving tentacles, from plankton to crabs, sea stars, and fish. An anemone drags its prey into its mouth, which is the only opening into and out of its stomach. Some anemones reproduce by splitting themselves apart, creating new anemones that will grow together in large colonies. The new anemones are called "clones" and each one looks exactly like the other.

The shape of an anemone's tentacles indicates what it likes to eat. Anemones that eat plankton have fine tentacles that can easily grab plankton floating in the current. Anemones that hunt larger animals, such as crabs, sea stars, and fish, have stubby tentacles that are strong enough to grasp their prey.

In the sand between the rocks a tube anemone is feeding on plankton. It plucks food particles out of the water with long, thin tentacles. A large, bright orange sea slug approaches the anemone. Called a rainbow nudibranch, this is a snail that has no shell. With a sudden strike, the nudibranch leaps upon the anemone, biting off the anemone's tentacles. The anemone draws back into its tube and the nudibranch goes with it, feeding as it goes.

Left: Rainbow nudibranchs may lay their egg strings around an anemone so the eggs will be protected from hungry crabs and fishes by the anemone's stinging tentacles.

Far left: Rainbow nudibranchs don't eat entire anemones, just a few tentacles. As the nudibranch eats, it stores the stinging cells from the anemone in the gills on its back. Afterwards, any fish that attacks the nudibranch will be stung by these cells.

Left: The rainbow nudibranch leaps into the mouth of the anemone, holds onto the tentacles as the anemone withdraws into its tube, and feeds on the stinging tentacles as it is drawn farther into the tube anemone.

Above: The spanish shawl nudibranch looks like it is on fire. The bright colors warn of its bad taste.

The chromodoris nudibranch has brightly colored stripes. It dines on the blue cobalt sponge that covers rocks.

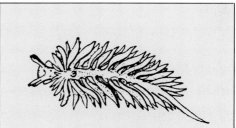

Sea Slugs

Sea slugs are also called nudibranchs (noo-di-branks), which means "naked gills." Unlike other marine animals, their gills are on the outside of their bodies, rather than on the inside. Nudibranchs have sensory horns that they use to touch and smell. They come in many shapes and brilliant colors. Scientists think that the bright colors warn potential predators of their bad taste. Many nudibranchs are protected from their predators by stinging cells or bad-tasting chemicals which they have absorbed from animals that they've eaten, such as anemones and sponges. While most nudibranchs are only a few inches long, some species can grow to be a foot in length.

Suddenly the sea otter appears, diving to the ocean floor. It digs through the rocks to find another of its favorite foods: abalone. The otter surprises a small octopus hiding under a rock. The octopus quickly shoots a spurt of ink, which hangs in the water and tricks the otter into grabbing the inky shape instead of the octopus. Instead of jetting away, the octopus changes color, and spreads out its arms to look like a piece of drift kelp. The sea otter can't find the octopus, even though the octopus is right in front of it!

Above: Sea otters are skillful underwater swimmers, but must surface for air after two minutes.

Far left: The octopus can change shape, color, and even texture in a split-second.

Left: The octopus disguises itself to look like a piece of drift kelp.

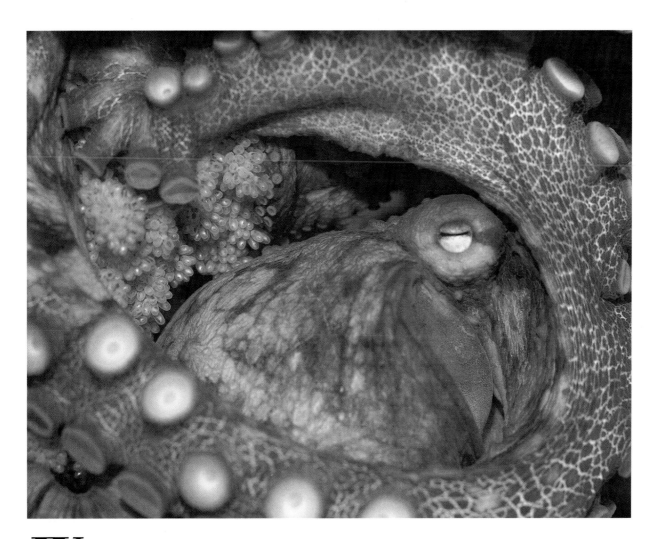

The female octopus is one of the world's most devoted parents, and does not eat until her eggs hatch. Soon after they hatch she dies.

Below left: A brood of octopus eggs takes six weeks to hatch.

Below: When baby octopi hatch, they are no bigger than a fingernail.

*W*hen the otter leaves, the octopus glides under another rock, seeking the safety of a dark cave. However, it is quickly chased away by an angry female octopus who is brooding her eggs inside the cave.

*F*arther out in the deep blue distance of the open ocean, several large shapes pass by. They are dolphins, moving like rockets through the water. They have discovered a school of anchovies. Calling to each other with high-pitched squeaks and whistles, the dolphins circle the large school. Frightened fish on the edges of the school crowd closer to the center, and the entire school becomes confused. Taking turns, each of the dolphins makes a pass through the mass, grabbing several mouthfuls of fish. Then, as quickly as they came, the dolphins are gone, and the anchovies once again swim together in a school.

Dolphins are highly social animals that usually travel together in large groups called pods.

28

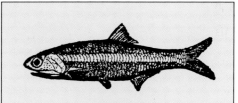

Anchovy

Anchovies swim together in large schools, sometimes consisting of thousands of fish. Each fish in the school somehow senses how the other members of the school are going to move, allowing the group to move together as a single unit. Some predators may mistake the school for a single large animal, and so keep their distance. Others may become confused by the thousands of fish in a school and have a hard time hunting a single fish in the crowd.

*E*ven deeper in the seemingly bottomless water, sharks are constantly moving in search of prey. A mako shark speeds past a slow-moving blue shark. On the mako's dorsal fin trail long strings of copepod eggs. With a quick twist of its tail, the mako shark speeds off into the distance.

Above left: Blue sharks are slow-moving and curious, hardly like the ferocious monsters portrayed in the movies. A diver is lucky to see one.

Left: Anchovies travel together in large groups called schools.

After mating, each female squid lays an egg case on the sandy ocean floor. Each egg case contains two hundred eggs.

Below left: Its long, flat shape helps the angel shark blend into the sand.

Below: After mating and laying their eggs the exhausted squid die.

With oncoming darkness, an entirely different set of animals emerges. At the edge of the kelp bed, a huge gathering of squid is making its way to shallow waters, where they will mate and lay their eggs on the sand. This huge gathering only happens a few nights a year. Crabs and anemones capture the squid, exhausted from a night of mating and laying eggs. An angel shark lies flat in the sand. Its long, flat shape helps it blend into the sand, just like a stingray. When a squid passes by, the angel shark lunges out of its hiding place and gulps down the squid.

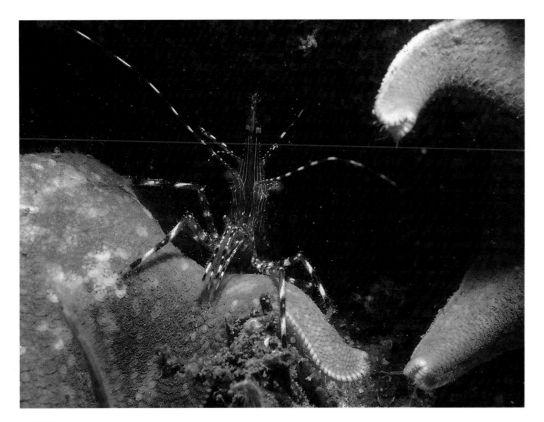

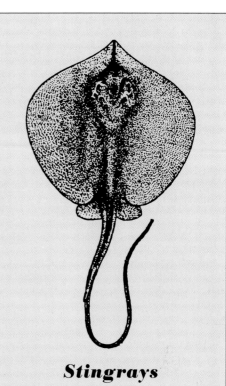

Coonstripe shrimp hide during the day and emerge at night when it is dark.

The electric ray is capable of generating up to two hundred volts of electricity.

Coonstripe shrimp make their way from their hiding places, as do kelp crabs, sea cucumbers, and nocturnal fishes such as the electric ray. The shrimp and crabs climb to the tops of small plants and rocks where they will sit through the night, sifting through the water for food. In the dark waters above, hundreds of bat rays gather to dance together in the last light of day.

Stingrays

More people are seriously hurt by stingrays than by any other creature of the sea. Each stingray has a long, sharp barb at the base of its tail which it uses to defend itself. Since stingrays like sandy areas close to the shore, they are often stepped on by people wading in the shallow water. If stepped on, a stingray can inflict a painful and poisonous wound with its barbed tail.

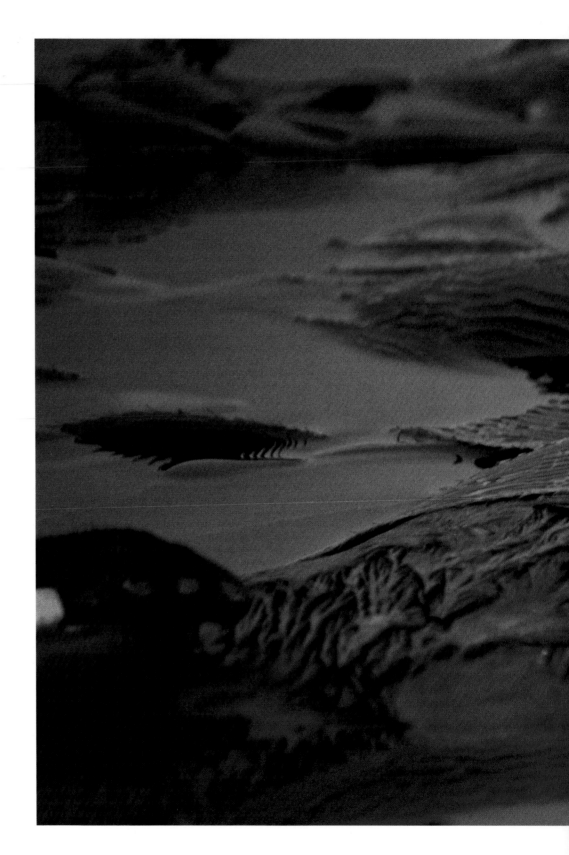

Back on the water's surface, the otter once again rolls in the kelp, making its bed for the night. Rocked to sleep by the gently rolling waves, the otter sleeps entwined in the kelp to keep from drifting away. This way the otter will awake in the same place ready to start another new day.

At the end of each day, the sea otter winds itself in long strands of kelp. This keeps the otter from floating away while it sleeps through the night.

About the Photographer

When I was six years old, I knew that I wanted to become a marine biologist. As a teenager, I spent my summers snorkeling off the coast of Florida. In college, deluged with the advice of others, I studied engineering rather than marine biology. But my thoughts kept wandering to tropical coral reefs. After working for a short time as an engineer, I took a job as a research diver with the Smithsonian Tropical Research Institute in the San Blas Islands of Panama.

Although I was an experienced diver, I had no knowledge of underwater photography, so I bought as many books as I could find on the subject. Then, with a relatively simple camera system, I embarked on an adventure that was to become my career. The island that I lived on consisted of one hundred square feet of sand, and the researchers lived in bamboo and plywood huts right above the water. Diving every day, I came to know the reefs and their inhabitants intimately, and I learned to make careful studies of the habits and behaviors of marine life.

Now I earn my living doing the things I dreamed of as a boy. I've dived all over the world, from the Arctic to the tropics, and have learned far more about the wonders of the ocean than I ever could have imagined. Photography and learning about ocean wildlife have become my passion and my career, and for me it is an exciting and fulfilling occupation.

Underwater Photography

Most of the photographs in this book were taken in Monterey Bay off the coast of California. When planning a dive, the first thing I do is find a fellow diver to help with the many tasks that are part of the job. Then the photography equipment must be collected and put into working condition.

I use two types of cameras in my work: a Nikonos which is designed for underwater use, and a land camera encased in a waterproof housing. I use different lenses, ranging from a wide-angle lens for large subjects to a macro lens for focusing on small subjects. To light my subjects, I use underwater strobe lights, or flashes. As I explore, I look for colors as well as striking patterns. In order to see colors in the deep, dark waters, I often use a powerful underwater flashlight.

The time I spend underwater is very valuable, and usually too short. I prefer diving a particular reef several times. In this way, I learn about the behavior of the animals who live there — where an octopus has its lair, or where a wolf eel hides. Once I find a subject, I photograph it in its habitat in a number of different compositions. After fifteen years of diving, underwater life continues to fascinate me. Each day I learn something new about my business — about natural history, about people, about technology, and about diving.

Glossary

algae: simple plants, which can range in size from small, one-celled organisms to large, many-celled forms such as the giant kelp, or *Macrocystis*.

amphipod: any of a large group of small crustaceans. Amphipods are usually very small and form the food of many baleen whales.

atmosphere: the air, or the gases which surround Earth.

baleen: a horny material which hangs from the upper jaw of certain whales, and which is used to filter plankton, krill, and other food particles from the water.

bell: the top part of a jellyfish, inside of which is the gut or body cavity. Surrounding the bell is a ring of tentacles.

blade: the leaflike part of the giant kelp plant.

blubber: a layer of fat in most marine mammals which keeps the mammal warm.

brooding: the act of caring for the eggs or young.

camouflage: the colors and patterns that help a plant or an animal blend into its surroundings.

canopy: the uppermost, branching layer of a forest.

cartilage: an elastic tissue that is softer than bone.

cilia: hairlike projections from the body of comb jellies and other small invertebrates, which are used to propel the animal through water.

clone: a copy of an original form. Anemones often form clones of themselves by splitting apart to form two new individuals, each one identical to the other.

coelenterate: a group of invertebrate animals which includes corals, sea anemones, and jellyfishes. These animals are characterized by having a hollow center surrounded by a ring of stinging tentacles.

comb jelly: a marine animal that looks like a jellyfish but is not related. Comb jellies have eights rows of combs (or plates) along the side of their bodies that are used to help them move through the water.

comet: a newly formed (or regenerated) sea star grown from the broken arm (or ray) or disc of an original sea star.

commensal relationship: a relationship in which two organisms live with, on, or in each other, without injury to either.

current: a movement or flow of water in a certain direction.

deforestation: the removal of forests or vegetation from land or an underwater area.

dorsal fin: the fin or finlike extension on the back of fish, whales, and dolphins.

drifter: any type of animal which lives in the open ocean, and flows along with the currents rather than swimming under its own power.

echinoderms: a group of invertebrate animals which includes starfish, sand dollars, sea cucumbers, and sea urchins. These animals are radially symmetrical, which means that their bodies are arranged around a central point, and look the same on all sides.

egg string: a mass of eggs which are laid by an animal.

extinct: no longer living.

fertilize: to cause eggs from a female to become capable of producing offspring.

filter-feeding: the act of removing food particles from a mass of water.

gills: the respiratory organs of marine animals which remove oxygen from the water, allowing the animals to breathe.

groom: to tend carefully; to make hair or fur neat and tidy.

habitat: the native environment of an animal or plant.

herd: any large number of animals which travel and live together as a group.

holdfast: the bottom, root-like part of the giant kelp plant that anchors the kelp.to the ocean floor.

insulate: to protect or surround with material; to stop or reduce the loss of heat.

intruder: something that enters without permission or by force.

invertebrate: any animal without a backbone, or vertebrae.

kelp bed: a group of kelp growing together, which may form a forest of kelp.

kelp canopy: the tops of kelp plants floating on the surface of the water.

larva: the early life form of insects and many ocean animals, from the time they leave the egg until the next growth stage.

mantle: the soft outer body wall that lines the shells of mollusks.

marine mammal: a warm-blooded animal that gives birth to live young and lives in the ocean. Marine mammals include dolphins, whales, seals, sea lions, and sea otters.

mollusk: any invertebrate animal (such as a snail, bivalve, squid, or octopus) with a soft body and usually having a shell that encloses the body.

nocturnal: active at night.

parasite: a living thing that spends its life on or in another living thing. A parasite gets its food from other organisms, often harming the host animal in the process.

pelagic: living or growing in the open ocean, as opposed to the shore or reefs.

photosynthesis: the process whereby plants convert the energy of sunlight into food.

plankton: tiny, floating plants and animals of the ocean. Plankton forms the base of the food chain for all animals that live in the ocean.

pod: a group of animals clustered together, such as seals, dolphins, and whales.

population explosion: a sudden increase in the number of a particular species of animal.

predator: an animal that captures and eats other animals.

prey: an animal which is eaten by another animal.

primitive: very simple; of early times.

radula: the row of file-like teeth found in snails and other mollusks.

ray: one of the branches or arms of a starfish, or one of the hard rods in the fin of a fish.

reef: a ridge of sand or a group of rocks near the surface of water.

regeneration: the process where a body part grows back.

school: a large group of fish that swims and feeds together as a single unit.

sea urchin barren: an area where sea urchins have grown uncontrollably and eaten all the kelp and other algae on the ocean bottom.

spine: a stiff, sharp-pointed growth on animals or plants.

stipe: the middle part of the kelp plant, which consists of long, thin, hollow tubes.

suction cup: the part of a cling-fish, octopus, or squid which the animal uses to hold onto a surface.

symbiosis: a relationship in which two organisms mutually benefit from each other.

tentacles: the appendages (or arms) of invertebrate animals, used as organs of touch: feelers.

territory: an area occupied and defended by an animal, often containing a nest site and food range.

tide: the rise and fall of the waters of the ocean caused by the pull of gravity and the Earth's rotation.

tunicates: invertebrate animals that have sac-like bodies enclosed in a thick membrane or tunic and possess some vertebrate characteristics, such as a primitive backbone (the notochord).

Index

In the course of his worldwide travels, **Norbert Wu** has been bitten by sharks, run over by an iceberg, stung nearly to death by sea wasps, and trapped in an underwater cave. He has photographed underwater in nearly every conceivable locale, ranging from the freezing waters of the Arctic open ocean to the coral reefs of the tropics. His writing and photography have appeared in numerous books, films, and magazines, including *Audubon, Harper's, International Wildlife, Le Figaro, National Geographic, Omni, Outside, Smithsonian,* and the covers of *GEO, Natural History, Time,* and *Terre Sauvage* magazines. The author and photographer of seven books on wildlife and photography, his photographic library of marine and topside wildlife is one of the most comprehensive in the world.

Also from Chronicle Books and Norbert Wu: *Creeps from the Deep,* written by Leighton Taylor